Contents

What is Kayaking and Canoeing?

Whether you want the relaxation of paddling along a quiet river, or the excitement of bouncing through white water in a tiny boat, kayaking and canoeing are sports that have something for everyone.

Just Add Water

You can kayak or canoe on pretty much any river or stream, on lakes, lagoons and in the ocean. All you need is a boat, some basic safety gear and a little bit of knowledge to start enjoying yourself on the water. It is important to make sure that you have enough experience to deal with the conditions, though. It would be extremely dangerous to paddle out into giant waves or a rushing whitewater river for your first lesson.

The Difference between Kayaking and Canoeing

Kayaking and canoeing are both done in the same kinds of boat, usually paddled by one or two people. But there is one crucial difference between them. A kayaker uses a long paddle that has a blade (the wide, flat section that is used to move you through the water) at both ends. A canoeist uses a short paddle that has a blade only at one end. This difference means the boats have to be paddled in different ways.

Whitewater kayaking: this is kayaking, rather than canoeing, because the paddler is using a two-bladed paddle.

Kayaking
and Canoeing
Yvonne Thorpe

W
FRANKLIN WATTS
LONDON • SYDNEY

First published in 2009 by
Franklin Watts
338 Euston Road
London NW1 3BH

Franklin Watts Australia
Level 17/207 Kent Street
Sydney NSW 2000

Series editor: Jeremy Smith
Art director: Jonathan Hair

**Series designed and created for
Franklin Watts by Storeybooks.**
Designer: Rita Storey
Editor: Nicola Edwards
Photography: Tudor Photography,
   Banbury and Jon Hare
www.fullfatphotography.com

A CIP catalogue record for this book
is available from the British Library.

Dewey classification: 797.1'22
ISBN 978 0 7496 8862 2
Printed in China

Franklin Watts is a division of Hachette
Children's Books, an Hachette UK company.
www.hachette.co.uk

Note: At the time of going to press, the statistics in this book were up to date. However, it is possible because of the kayakers' and canoeists' ongoing participation in the sport that some of these may now be out of date.

Picture credits
© Wolfram's Adventure Photography/Alamy p18; BigStock p27; Getty Images p20, Michael Kappeler/AFP/Getty Images p24 and Mlanden Antonov/AFP/Getty Images p25; Jon Hare pp.15, 16, 17 and 19; istock pp6, 9 (top and middle), 18, 21, 22, 23 and 26; Tudor Photography pp1, 2, 3, 7, 8, 9 (bottom), 10, 11, 12, 13 and 14.

Cover images: Tudor Photography, Banbury.

All photos posed by models. Thanks to Liam Kirkham, Alice Murphy, Dom Murphy, Padraig Rooney and Sophie Rooney.

The Publisher would like to thank Banbury and District Canoe Club for their help.

WARNING:
This book is not a substitute for learning from a skilled coach, which is the only safe way to learn kayaking and canoeing techniques.

Getting Started

It does not need to cost much to have your first go at kayaking or canoeing. Most canoe clubs run 'taster' sessions to allow people the chance to try out the sport alongside experienced paddlers. If you enjoy it, the next step might be to sign up for a course before investing in your own boat, paddle and safety kit. Find a club through the International Canoe Federation (you can find the website address on page 29).

Competitions

Most kayakers and canoeists take part in the sport for fun, but there is also a big competition scene. There are two main types of contest: sprint racing and white water (see pages 22–25). The pinnacle of competition is the Olympic Games, where every four years the world's best paddlers get the chance to race each other.

Young kayakers (in front) and a canoeist (behind) at their local canoe club. Who knows – maybe one of them will go on to become an Olympic champion!

Types of Boat

For many beginners, a basic, all-round boat is ideal. Once you become a bit more experienced you will find that, whatever kind of paddling you want to do, there is a special type of boat to help you do it.

Bottom Shape

Bottom shape is one of the most important design features in a boat. A flat bottom is difficult to balance in, and tips over easily. But it will also be easy to turn quickly. A boat with a deeper bottom (usually V-shaped if you look at it head-on) will be the opposite. It will be stable, and easy to balance in, but harder to turn.

Width

A boat's width affects the way it paddles, especially its acceleration. A relatively wide boat gets up to top speed quickly, so is ideal for whitewater paddling in rivers or the sea. A longer, thinner outline is usually slower to get up to speed, but will probably be easier to keep moving once it has got there. This makes this type of boat best for longer distances.

Length and Volume

A boat's volume dictates how well it floats. Heavier paddlers need boats with more volume (the amount of space inside), so that they do not sink too low in the water. Usually, longer boats have more volume than shorter ones.

Whitewater Boat

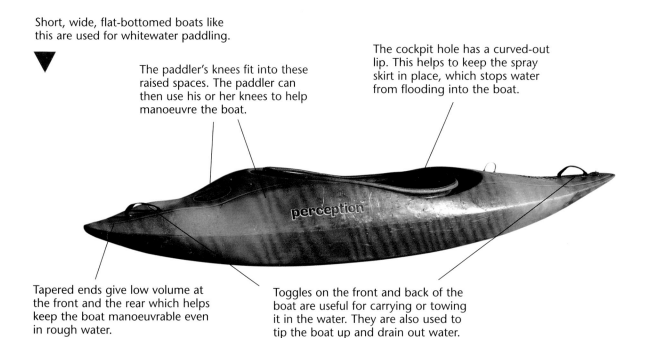

Short, wide, flat-bottomed boats like this are used for whitewater paddling.

The paddler's knees fit into these raised spaces. The paddler can then use his or her knees to help manoeuvre the boat.

The cockpit hole has a curved-out lip. This helps to keep the spray skirt in place, which stops water from flooding into the boat.

Tapered ends give low volume at the front and the rear which helps keep the boat manoeuvrable even in rough water.

Toggles on the front and back of the boat are useful for carrying or towing it in the water. They are also used to tip the boat up and drain out water.

Paddle Weight

The most important thing about a paddle is how much it weighs. A lighter paddle is much less tiring to use than a heavy one. Many top kayakers and canoeists use carbon fibre paddles, which are light and very strong. Paddles are also sometimes made of plastic, fibreglass or even wood.

A touring boat in action.

Touring Boat

Touring boats like this are used for long-distance trips, especially at sea.

Toggles on each end help with carrying, dragging the boat up the beach and draining it of water.

The cockpit lip holds the spray skirt in place.

The high front helps the boat cut through choppy waves without being swamped.

Elasticated webbing is useful for tucking clothes and other luggage underneath (as long as they do not need to stay dry!).

The rudder is connected to paddles inside the boat. The paddler can push on these with his or her feet to help steer one way or the other.

Open boats such as this one have plenty of room, and are ideal for fishing or just messing about on calmer water.

Open Boat

The boat is open to the weather, so water gets inside easily.

Single-bladed paddle

Seats for paddlers

Clothing and Equipment

Kayaking and canoeing are both potentially dangerous activities. Apart from the risk of drowning, there are also dangers from cold water and the heat of the sun. Having the right clothing and equipment makes paddling much safer.

Killer Cold

One of a paddler's biggest enemies is cold. Even on a hot day, the water can be chilly. Inevitably, water runs down your wrists from the paddles, and sprays onto your face and body. Staying warm and dry inside a wetsuit top, or a special waterproof with warm gear underneath, protects you from the cold. Without this protective clothing, paddlers risk hypothermia – when the body's temperature falls to dangerously low temperatures.

Deadly Heat

Almost as dangerous as the cold is the heat from the sun. Paddlers should wear sunscreen and cover the head and as much skin as possible with clothing. Otherwise they risk sunburn, dehydration and sunstroke. Sunburn is very painful; dehydration and sunstroke are both very serious. They can leave you feeling weak, dizzy and confused – far from ideal when you are taking part in a dangerous sport.

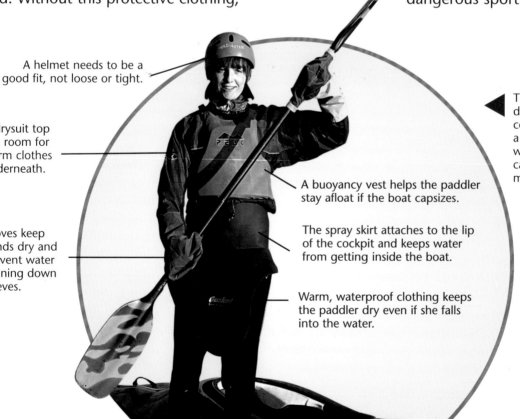

A helmet needs to be a good fit, not loose or tight.

A drysuit top has room for warm clothes underneath.

Gloves keep hands dry and prevent water running down sleeves.

This kayaker is dressed for cold conditions. Even a dunking in chilly water would not cause her too much distress.

A buoyancy vest helps the paddler stay afloat if the boat capsizes.

The spray skirt attaches to the lip of the cockpit and keeps water from getting inside the boat.

Warm, waterproof clothing keeps the paddler dry even if she falls into the water.

Safety Gear

The two most important pieces of safety gear are a paddler's helmet and buoyancy vest. The vest keeps you afloat if you fall out of your boat. The helmet protects your head from bangs that could knock you unconscious. Both are especially important in whitewater paddling. In white water, a paddler is more likely to capsize, be knocked about in the water, or have to swim to shore. The risk

of banging your head on the boat, rocks and other obstacles makes a helmet essential.

> ### Top Tip
> **Make sure you drink plenty while paddling, to avoid dehydration. Most people need to drink between seven and ten average-sized glasses of water a day – more if they do hard exercise.**

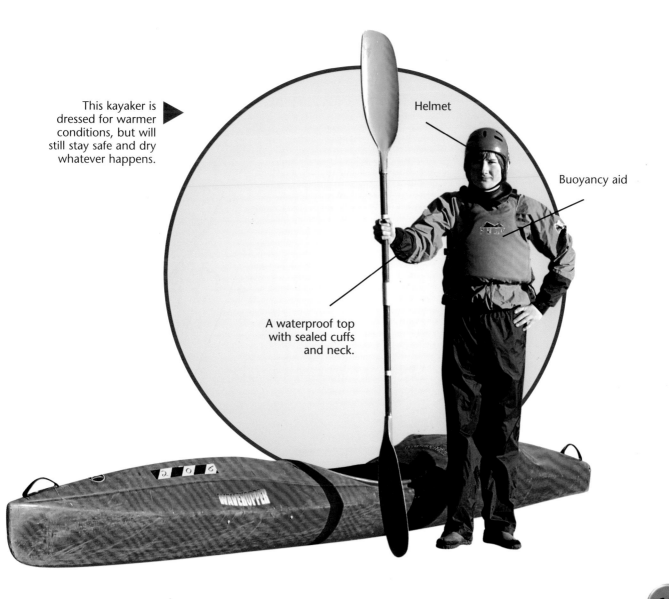

This kayaker is dressed for warmer conditions, but will still stay safe and dry whatever happens.

Helmet

Buoyancy aid

A waterproof top with sealed cuffs and neck.

Launching

Before you can paddle a kayak or a canoe, you have to launch it – in other words, get in and get it safely afloat! Usually this is done either from a beach or from a jetty. There are different techniques depending on whether you are launching from a jetty, a steep riverbank, a shallow riverbank or a beach.

Learning to Launch

The best way to learn how to launch a boat is to practise in calm, shallow water at first.

This allows beginners to get used to the shifts in balance that happen as they get into the boat. Of course, if they get it wrong they get wet – but in shallow water that shouldn't be a disaster. Even experienced whitewater paddlers prefer to launch into a quiet eddy, before paddling out into the bumpy river.

Fasten the Spray Skirt

One big advantage of launching into quiet water is that it gives you a chance to fasten your spray skirt as soon as you get in the boat. Trying to do this later on is very tricky, and best avoided.

Launching a Boat from a Riverbank

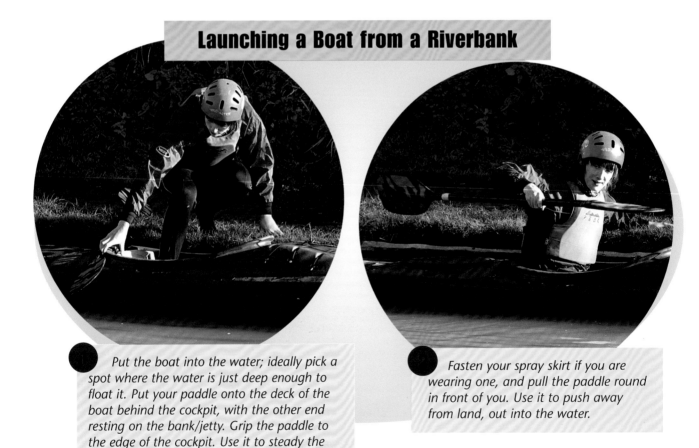

Put the boat into the water; ideally pick a spot where the water is just deep enough to float it. Put your paddle onto the deck of the boat behind the cockpit, with the other end resting on the bank/jetty. Grip the paddle to the edge of the cockpit. Use it to steady the boat as you get in.

Fasten your spray skirt if you are wearing one, and pull the paddle round in front of you. Use it to push away from land, out into the water.

Launching a Boat from a Jetty

1. *Balance the boat with the cockpit a little behind the edge of the jetty. Get in and fasten your spray skirt. Lean forwards to tip the boat in.*

2. *As the boat enters the water, lean back to help bring the front up, and start paddling.*

Extreme Launching

Experienced paddlers are able to launch their boats from some pretty extreme places. They slide their boats off the ends of jetties (as above), or from the tops of rocks and bridges, for example. This kind of launch is not recommended for beginners!

Launching an Open Boat from a Jetty

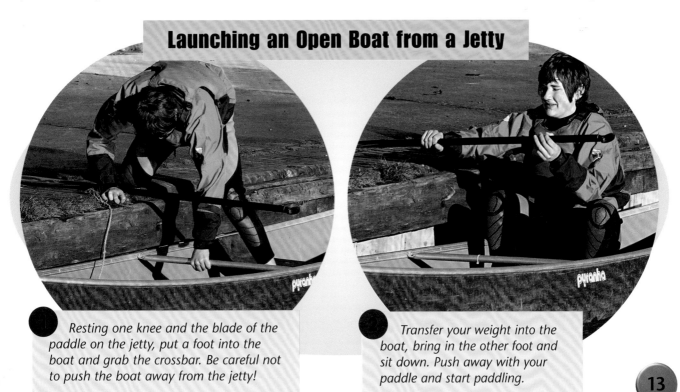

1. *Resting one knee and the blade of the paddle on the jetty, put a foot into the boat and grab the crossbar. Be careful not to push the boat away from the jetty!*

2. *Transfer your weight into the boat, bring in the other foot and sit down. Push away with your paddle and start paddling.*

Paddling and Steering

Paddling technique is the difference between kayaking and canoeing. Kayakers use a long paddle with blades at each end. Canoeists use a short, single-bladed oar. The principles of turning are the same for both.

Paddling Technique – Canoeing

In canoeing, the paddler has to dip in a single blade on either side of the boat. This means twisting your body from side to side, to paddle left-right, left-right. This can be done from a sitting position, but racing canoeists kneel in the boat.

Paddling Technique – Kayaking

Kayakers have no need to twist their body from side to side, because they have a paddle with two blades. The blades are set at an angle to each other, usually about 80°. To go in a straight line, the paddler takes strokes on alternate sides of the boat.

Paddling in a Kayak

In kayaking, the paddler has to roll his or her wrists between each stroke, so that the angled blades catch the water properly.

1 The paddler reaches forward with her left arm, dips the blade in the water, and pulls back strongly. As this blade comes out of the water, the opposite blade is moving forwards and down.

2 The paddler rolls her right wrist forwards, so that the right-hand blade goes into the water smoothly, and repeats the stroke. The left-hand blade passes easily through the air as it moves forwards.

Turning

To adjust course while keeping up speed, paddlers put in more strokes on one side than the other. The more strokes they take on one side, the faster the boat will turn.

To make a sharper turn, paddlers take a backwards stroke. This is a bit like throwing out an anchor on one side. The boat slows down, and pivots around the paddle.

Turning

1 *Paddling with the left blade pushes the boat round to the right. Using only the left blade makes a sharper turn; taking a half stroke with the right blade afterwards will allow a slight change of direction.*

2 *Paddling forwards with the right blade will push the boat gradually round to the left. With experience it is possible to use your hips to add to the turn by pivoting to the right.*

3 *Paddling back with the left blade brings the boat round sharply to the left.*

3 *A back-paddle with the right blade will begin a sharp right turn.*

Safety

Kayaking and canoeing are dangerous sports, especially in white water or surf. It is important to have the right safety equipment, and to know what to do if an accident happens and you get tipped out of the boat.

A Quick Decision

If the boat capsizes, a paddler has a choice about what to do. Inexperienced paddlers usually have to do an emergency escape, getting out of the boat then towing it to shore. Experienced paddlers may be able to do an Eskimo roll – the skill of quickly flipping the boat back upright without having to get out of it. There is more about the Eskimo roll on page 19.

Making an Emergency Escape

Getting out of an overturned boat quickly is a crucial skill. Without it, you risk being trapped underwater with the boat holding you in place. ▶

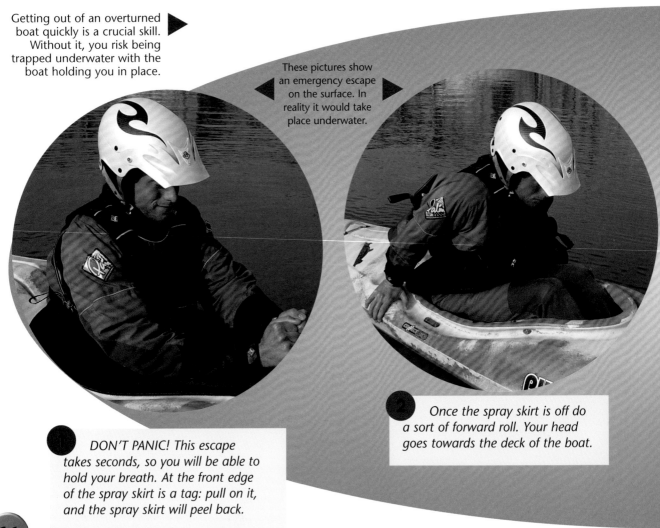

These pictures show an emergency escape on the surface. In reality it would take place underwater.

1 DON'T PANIC! This escape takes seconds, so you will be able to hold your breath. At the front edge of the spray skirt is a tag: pull on it, and the spray skirt will peel back.

2 Once the spray skirt is off do a sort of forward roll. Your head goes towards the deck of the boat.

Underwater Hazards

In any water there may be hazards lurking beneath the surface. Rocks, shallow areas and submerged logs can all tip you out of the boat. Sometimes the water surface gives clues as to what's underneath it: experienced paddlers know how to look out for these clues (see pages 20–21 for more information).

In the Water

If paddlers somehow get separated from their boat, they need to avoid underwater obstacles. Getting caught up in underwater roots or trapped against a rock in a fast-flowing river can be disastrous. Floating on your back, with your feet up and hands crossed over your chest, is the safest position.

Top Tip

ALWAYS make sure the pull-tag on your spray skirt is on the outside, so that you will be able to get hold of it in an emergency.

3 *You can help yourself out of the boat by pushing on the sides of the cockpit. Your body and legs will follow your body out of the boat.*

4 *Once you are at the surface, grab one of the boat's carrying toggles. Get hold of your paddle, then tow your boat to dry land.*

Whitewater Paddling

Whitewater paddling is one of the toughest, most exciting ways to go kayaking or canoeing. It takes place on fast-flowing rivers. Rocks and other underwater obstacles make the surface of the water bumpy and tricky for paddling.

Grades of White Water

Some whitewater rivers are harder to paddle down than others. Most stretches of white water on a river are given a grade to show how dangerous they are. The higher the grade number, the more dangerous the river will be.

• A Grade 1 section is relatively easy to paddle, with few hazards.
• A Grade 6 river is the toughest grade. Paddling a Grade 6 river would be extremely dangerous even for an expert.

Changes to the River

Rivers become harder or easier to paddle down depending on how much water is flowing. Mountain rivers may need heavy rainfall before there is enough water to paddle down them at all. Other rivers may be hazardous only when there has been little rain. It is important to find out before setting off down a river what the conditions are going to be.

This kayaker has let himself in for some extreme whitewater action! Waterfalls like this one are very dangerous and for experienced paddlers only.

Safety – the Eskimo Roll

The most important safety technique in white water is the Eskimo roll, a quick way of getting the boat upright without getting out. The roll gets its name from people who live in the frozen north. If their kayaks tipped over, they had to get out of the water within seconds or freeze to death. The technique is just as useful for paddlers who don't want to bounce their way down a river upside-down.

Eskimo Roll

1 *Capsize! In white water, the paddler needs to get the boat upright as soon as possible.*

2 *The paddler gets ready to roll back upright. He gets the paddle into a position where he can pull against it.*

3 *Pulling on the paddle to get the boat turning, the paddler uses a twist of the hips to help it on its way.*

4 *Phew! Now he can safely start paddling again.*

Reading the River

Expert kayakers and canoeists can 'read' the surface of a river. The waves and swirls on the surface of white water indicate what is beneath.

White water occurs when a river flows quickly over underwater obstacles. The shapes and waves that appear on the surface give clues about what is underneath.

Paddlers can use these clues to plot a safe course through the white water.

Chutes

A chute is a path of smooth water flowing through a whitewater part of the river. The chute is usually the safest way to get through a whitewater section. You can usually tell the start of a chute because there will be V-shaped ripples pointing downstream.

The paddler in the orange boat is taking a safe course down a 'chute' of water.

Paddling a Safe Course

At the top, he aims for the centre of the chute, where the water is likely to be deepest. He paddles into it, as a bit of speed helps the boat hold to the right line.

Halfway down, the water carries the boat along. There is often no chance to paddle here, so lift the paddle up to keep it clear of obstacles. As soon as possible, the paddler digs in and speeds the boat away from the bottom of the chute, where there may be dangerous currents.

This paddler is resting in an 'eddy'. Places to rest such as this can come in very handy on a long whitewater section.

Tyler Bradt

Nationality: USA

Bradt is one of the stars of extreme kayaking. He first sat in a boat at the age of six, and has gone on to make his name by paddling over breathtakingly steep waterfalls. At the age of 21, Bradt set the world record (32.6m/107ft, in September 2007) for a waterfall plunge in a kayak, at Alesandra Falls in Canada's Northwest Territory.

Eddies

An eddy is an area of calm water. Eddies are usually found downstream of obstacles such as large rocks, which act as a barrier to the river's flow. Sometimes eddies are also found in areas away from the main flow of water. The water in an eddy flows upstream. Pulling into an eddy can upset inexperienced paddlers – the front of their kayak goes upstream while the back is still going downstream!

Standing Waves

Standing waves are just what they sound like – waves that stand still, staying in the same place. Standing waves happen where fast-flowing water suddenly slows down. This happens because the river has suddenly become deeper or wider. Standing waves can sometimes show a good path through white water.

Underwater Rocks

V-shaped ripples pointing upstream, or smooth 'lumps' of water with white water downstream of them, are a clue that there is a rock lurking under the surface. Take another route!

21

Slalom and Wildwater

Slalom and wildwater racing are two types of whitewater competition. Both require extremely high levels of fitness, strength and skill. Slalom has featured as a sport in every Olympic Games since 1992.

Slalom Contests

Slalom has contests both for canoeists and kayakers, men and women (only men race canoe slalom at the Olympics). The paddlers have to navigate their way through a series of 'gates' (pairs of poles hanging down over the water) as quickly as possible. Sometimes they come at the gates heading downstream; other gates must be taken in an upstream direction. Touching one of the poles with the paddle or the body costs a time penalty, which is added to the time for the run.

The slalom canoeist turns in towards the gate and digs in on the left-hand side, driving the boat between the poles. This stroke has to be perfectly timed, so that the boat is driven through the gate and the paddle does not touch either of the poles.

▼

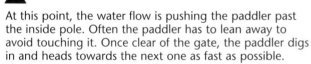
At this point, the water flow is pushing the paddler past the inside pole. Often the paddler has to lean away to avoid touching it. Once clear of the gate, the paddler digs in and heads towards the next one as fast as possible.

Slalom Courses

Major slalom competitions are run on artificial courses. The advantage of these is that the water flow and obstacles remain the same for every paddler. Between rounds, the water flow can be adjusted and obstacles moved to vary the course.

Wildwater Contests

Wildwater races are run on natural rivers. In wildwater, there are no gates. The only aim is to get down the river as fast as possible. The contests are open to canoe and kayak racers and to men and women.

Richard Fox

Born: May 6th, 1960

Nationality: British

Richard Fox is Britain's most successful slalom kayaker. He first sat in a boat at the age of 11, but it was another four years before he discovered slalom. Despite this late start, he went on to win the world slalom championship ten times. Sadly when Fox was at his peak in the 1980s, slalom was not part of the Olympic Games. After his competition career ended, he moved to Australia, where he works as a national coach.

Sprint Racing

Sprint kayaking and canoeing are a classic test of speed and endurance in a boat. Races normally last 200m, 500m or 1,000m, though in the Olympics only 500m and 1000m are raced. Sprint racing has been part of the Olympic Games since 1936.

Boat Design

Sprint kayaks and canoes have very specialised designs. The boats are surprisingly long: about the length a normal boat for two or three people would be. The boats are hard to paddle, as they are designed purely for speed on flat water.

Canoe Racing

At international level, only men take part in canoeing races. There are three categories of race: for single paddlers (known as C1), pairs (C2) and fours (C4). As with other flat-water sprint races, each paddler races in his own lane, separated from the others by a line of buoys. Leaving your lane is not allowed and results in the paddler being disqualified.

The Chinese sprint C2 (two-man canoeing) team putting in a big effort as they near the finish at the 2008 Beijing Olympics.

2004 FES **Birgit Fischer**   Carolin Le

German Birgit Fischer and Carolin Leonhardt power to finish second in the Women's K2 class 500m final at the 2004 Olympic Games in Athens.

Paddling Technique

Canoe sprint racers kneel on the knee that's on the side they are paddling. They do not paddle on both sides. In the C1 class, this means that the boat is always paddled on one side only, so the racers have to use a special technique to keep the boat from moving in circles. This is called the 'J-stroke': at the end of the stroke, the paddler pushes the blade out and away from the boat, which stops it turning. In the C2 class, the racers paddle on opposite sides.

Race Classes – Kayaking

Kayaking races are open both to men and women. As in canoeing, there are races for single (K1), double (K2) and four-person (K4) crews.

Birgit Fischer

Born: February 25th, 1962

Nationality: German

Fischer is one of the greatest 500-metre sprint kayakers ever. (Sprint kayakers race in a straight line down a measured course.) Born in what was then East Germany, she has been both the youngest (at 18) and the oldest (at 42) Olympic kayak champion.

• In total, Fischer has won eight Olympic gold medals at seven different Olympic Games. She missed one Games, in 1984, because it was boycotted by the former East Germany.

• Fischer has also won an incredible 27 world championship titles.

Surf Kayaking

Surf kayaking is one of the most exciting kinds of paddling. It is possible to canoe in waves – in Hawaii, for example, traditional boats with several paddlers are popular surf craft. But most people prefer to use kayaks because of the extra speed and turning ability they offer.

Types of Surf Boat

There are two main types of surf boat: open and closed:

- Closed boats are like the kayaks that are used on rivers and lakes. The paddler sits inside the boat, with the cockpit sealed by a spray skirt.
- Open boats do not have a cockpit. Instead, the paddler sits on the boat. Sometimes they look similar to ordinary kayaks but with a large open cockpit. For surf, many people use a waveski, which is a bit like a very floaty, sit-down surfboard.

Wait for a Gap

Paddling out through the surf is tricky, especially in a closed boat. (On a waveski, if

This paddler is riding a waveski, a type of open kayak. The rider sits on top with his feet tucked into footstraps. The footstraps help the rider to lever the boat through turns.

▼

A kayak caught by a wave is pushed towards shore with tremendous force, so paddlers must take care not to hurt other water users.

Launching from a beach in small waves. The paddler sits the boat on the beach, just at the furthest extent of the waves. This makes it easy to get in and fasten the spray skirt. Then when a wave flows under the hull, the paddler wriggles the boat forwards using his hips until the water is deep enough to float.

you get tipped off all you have to do is climb back on, because the boat cannot fill with water.) The best technique is to wait for a gap in the waves, then sprint out. Waves come in sets, groups of between three and seven at a time. Wait for a gap between sets, and head for the horizon! If you do meet breaking waves, head straight for them to avoid being capsized.

Ocean Safety

The ocean can be a deadly place. Following a few rules helps to make sure you have fun in it, rather than ending up dangling from the rescue hoist of a rescue helicopter – or worse.

- Assume that you might have to rescue yourself. Never go out so far, or in such conditions, that you would not be able to make it back to shore.
- Never go out alone, and never exceed the ability of the weakest member of the group.
- When catching a wave, always remember that it is your job to avoid other people. People can never be 'in your way': YOU have to avoid THEM.
- If someone else is already riding a wave, let them get on with it. Dropping in on them would be dangerous – and rude!

Record Holders

Discipline:

Men's Slalom K1

Men's Slalom C1

Men's Slalom C2

Women's Slalom K1

Men's Sprint K1 1,000m

Men's Sprint K1 500m

Men's Sprint K2 1,000m

Men's Sprint K2 500m

Men's Sprint K4 1,000m

Men's Sprint C1 1,000m

Men's Sprint C1 500m

Men's Sprint C2 1,000m

Men's Sprint C2 500m

Women's Sprint K1 1,000m

Women's Sprint K1 500m

Women's Sprint K4 500m

Champion:

A. Grimm, Germany

M. Martikan, Slovakia

Pavol & Peter Hochschorner, Slovakia

E. Kaliska, Slovakia

T. Brabants, Great Britain

K. Wallace, Australia

M. Hollstein, A. Ihle, Germany

S. Craviotto, C. Perez, Spain

Belarus

A.S. Vajda, Hungary

M. Opalev, Russia

Andrei & Aleksandr Bahdanovich

G. Meng, W Wang, China

I. Osypenko-Radomska, Russia

K. Kovacs, N Janic, Hungary

Germany

Source: International Canoe Federation website
(www.canoeicf.com)

200m K1:	Women 0:38.970	Men 0:33.778
200m C1:		Men 0:38.363
500m K1:	Women 1:47.343	Men 1:35.630
500m C1:		Men 1:45.614
1,000m K1:	Women 3:52.983	Men 3:24.495
1,000m C1:		Men 3:46.201

Glossary

Blade The wide, flat section of a paddle that is used to move you through the water.

Bottom turn A turn made by surfers at the bottom of a wave, which allows them to start travelling along the wave instead of down it.

Boycotted To refuse to do something as a means of exerting pressure.

Capsize To turn over or upside-down in the water.

Closed Describes a boat in which the paddler sits inside the boat, usually with the cockpit sealed by a spray skirt.

Dehydration A dangerous lack of water inside the body.

Dropping in Catching a wave that someone else is already riding. In surfing, this is considered the height of rudeness, as well as being very dangerous.

East Germany The eastern part of the country that is now Germany, which between 1949 and 1990 was a separate country from West Germany. The two together are now a united country.

Eddy A still swirl of water.

Fibreglass A material made of glass fibres and resin – a sticky glue-like liquid that dries and hardens.

Hypothermia A state in which the body's temperature drops dangerously low.

Lagoon A calm, flat area of seawater that is partly surrounded by land.

Open Describes a boat that is open to the water and weather. Open boats do not have a cockpit; instead, the paddler sits on the boat.

Pivoting Turning around a central point.

Sets Groups of between three and seven waves that arrive one after the other.

Slalom A canoe and kayak event in which the racers have to steer through gates dotted along a whitewater course.

Stroke To dip the blade of a paddle into the water and use it to power a boat forwards.

Swamped Filled with water.

Unbroken Describes waves when they have no white water in front of them.

Volume The space inside an object. More space is higher volume; less space is lower volume.

White water Water that becomes bumpy and turbulent as it races over obstacles such as rocks, or waves that break as they reach a beach.

Wildwater White water that occurs naturally in rivers and streams.

Websites

www.canoeicf.com
The home page of the International Canoe Federation, which governs competition canoeing and kayaking around the world. As well as updates on contests, it has brief descriptions of the different types of canoeing and kayaking.

www.worldwaveski.com
The World Waveski Federation runs wave-riding competitions on ocean waves. You can use the site to find out if there's a big waveski event happening near you.

www.intraftfed.com
Rafting is many people's first taste of whitewater sports: find out more here. The International Rafting Federation governs whitewater rafting, in which several people together head down white water in an inflatable raft.

www.justcanoeit.com
A site campaigning for women to be allowed to take part in the same canoe and kayak events as men, at the Olympics and elsewhere.

Note to parents and teachers: every effort has been made by the Publishers to ensure that these websites are suitable for children, that they are of the highest educational value, and that they contain no inappropriate or offensive material. However, because of the nature of the Internet, it is impossible to guarantee that the contents of these sites will not be altered. We strongly advise that Internet access is supervised by a responsible adult.

Index